# Nature's Tresures

## A Colouring Book

**Dr. Anthonysamy David**

# Acknowledgement

I would like to extend my deepest appreciation to God almighty for providing the natural resources that are available. I also thank  Sebastian Kallupura, the Archbishop of Patna and Emirate Archbishop William D'Souza for their motivation. I also want to thank Fr. James George, the Archdiocese's Vicar General, and Fr. Amal, the treasurer of Patna Archdiocese. Along with i remember Fr. Agnello, the provincial of Pune Jesuit Province, and Fr. Stan, the Socius of Pune Province, for their constant support and care. Last but not least, I would like to thank all the social centre personnel, including the Director, Treasurer, program Coordinator and All the staff of the social centre, for their motivation.

This coloring book aims to raise awareness, particularly among students, about the vast and fragile natural resources that our planet provides. This book seeks to inspire young minds to recognize the importance of protecting and conserving these invaluable resources. People's commitment to environmental education has been empowering nature—not just a creative outlet but an important educational tool that underscores the responsibility we all share in preserving the Earth's bounty for future generations. I am sincerely grateful for all the people who contributed an unwavering passion for sustainability, which has been crucial in bringing this initiative to life.

Dr. Anthonysamy David
XINRM, Social Centre
Behind the Market Yard
Ahmednagar, Maharashtra 414001
danthonysamy@gmail.com

# Introduction to "Nature's Treasures: A Colouring Book.

Nature's Treasures: A Colouring Book is a thoughtfully crafted and educational experience that bridges the gap between artistic expression and environmental consciousness. With 50 intricately designed scenes, this colouring book showcases the breathtaking beauty and diversity of Earth's natural resources, from majestic forests and oceans to innovative renewable energy landscapes. Every page encourages not just mindfulness and relaxation but also creativity while subtly educating users about sustainability and conservation.

Ideal for nature enthusiasts of all ages, this book offers a tranquil, reflective journey through diverse ecosystems, inspiring a deeper connection to our planet. Explore the harmonious balance of nature and the significance of safeguarding these precious resources for future generations as you color each page. Whether for relaxation or personal growth, Nature's Treasures serves as both a creative outlet and a tool for raising environmental awareness, reminding us of our responsibility to safeguard the planet.